A souvenir guide

Dunster Castle
and Gardens

Somerset

National Trust

A Thousand Years of History

Dunster Castle has commanded this outstanding location atop the tor since the Middle Ages. It is the perfect site for a castle – visually impressive and easily defended. The castle, owned by only three families, has been transformed through the ages from fortress to family home.

If walls could talk

Dunster Castle is not as it may first appear. Originally built and fortified with defence in mind, it has changed greatly over the years, and now it tells a story of family life and a home full of warmth. Within forbidding walls is the story of the people who have lived here. They have left a legacy that includes 13th-century towers, a Jacobean mansion, rare 17th-century leather hangings, elaborately carved late 17th-century stairs and plasterwork ceilings, as well as all the comforts of a Victorian country home.

Fortunate escapes

Although it looks impregnable, the castle's fate has twice been in jeopardy. Oliver Cromwell ordered its destruction during the Civil War in 1650 but finally allowed the family living there at the time, the Luttrells, to retain their castle home. In 1949 the castle was sold to a property developer and its future hung in the balance. Fortunately Geoffrey Luttrell repurchased the castle in 1954, and in 1976 his son, Sir Walter, gave it to the National Trust. Walter's brother Julian maintains links with the National Trust and the home he grew up in, and he has generously shared some of his memories of what it was like to grow up in a castle.

'The castle is not just bricks and mortar, it's a living thing.'

Julian Luttrell, 2012

Below Dunster Castle surrounded by forest and countryside

The changing face of the castle

The long and eventful story of Dunster Castle is written on its walls. Its medieval masonry, Jacobean windows and Victorian doorways bear witness to changing functions and fashions, some more sympathetically introduced than others.

The de Mohuns arrived soon after William the Conquerer became King of England in 1066. William de Mohun was a knight who came from Normandy to help secure the area by establishing a castle on the site of a Saxon hill fort on the tor. This castle was later rebuilt in stone, although only the 13th-century gateway survives.

In 1376 the de Mohuns sold the castle to the Luttrell family, who were responsible for most of what we see at Dunster today. They built the gatehouse in 1420, created a Jacobean mansion in 1617, defended and saved the castle in the Civil War and updated it in Victorian times. Dunster Castle was a Luttrell family home until 1974, when Alys Luttrell, the last member of the family to live here, died.

A good deal
In 1376 Joan de Mohun sold Dunster Castle to Elizabeth Luttrell. Joan struck a deal which allowed her to live at Dunster until her death. This worked well for her as Elizabeth died before Joan, so she had the money from the sale and lived out her days in the castle.

Right above The views from the tor are largely unchanged but the castle has undergone transformations in its long history

Battered by war

Royalist armies surrounded the castle during the English Civil War (1642–51), when Thomas Luttrell and his wife Jane, both Parliamentarians, defended the castle. The family changed sides during the war and in 1645 the castle was again besieged, this time by Parliamentarians. Oliver Cromwell ordered the destruction of the castle and sent 200 men to demolish it. In 12 days in 1650 the exterior curtain walls were reduced to rubble. Fortunately the order was revoked and the castle itself was spared.

Fluctuating fortunes

The castle has seen times of prosperity and decline. Judicious marriages and careful estate management added to the family fortunes, but these were offset by bad luck, extravagant spending and difficult economic circumstances. At times the castle was a lively place, at others it was left empty as certain generations of the Luttrells chose to live at their other family estate at East Quantoxhead.

Left A view of Dunster from the south-east in the late 18th century, by William Tomkins

Above The Jacobean mansion in the early 18th century. Jacobean is the style associated with the reign of King James I of England (1603–25)

The faces that changed the castle

A number of Luttrells played a part in transforming and remodelling the castle. There were two major building periods – the first in the early 1600s and the second in the late 1800s – and both were by Georges.

In 1617 George Luttrell commissioned William Arnold to build a new house incorporating the lower ward's south tower and remaining medieval walling. An experienced draughtsman, Arnold had worked at Wadham College in Oxford and Montacute House in Somerset. At Dunster he created a fine Jacobean mansion with fashionable reception rooms and gave the north entrance a largely symmetrical appearance. Its plain walls, towers and battlements perhaps also reflected a Jacobean romantic taste for reviving chivalry and building sham castles – highly appropriate within the walls of a real medieval castle.

Mohair and silk beds

In 1680 Colonel Francis Luttrell, George's great grandson, married the beautiful and wealthy Dorset heiress, Mary Tregonwell. They spent enthusiastically, adding the carved staircase and a new dining room with elaborate plasterwork ceilings. A 1690 inventory lists silver, splendid pictures and luxurious beds hung with mohair, red and blue silks and yellow satin.

Below left George Luttrell, builder of Dunster

Below middle Colonel Francis Luttrell, by an unknown artist (Dining Room)

Below right Mary Tregonwell, by an unknown artist (Dining Room)

A woman's work

Colonel Francis died in 1690 and the estate passed to his brother Alexander (1663–1711). When he died, his young widow, Dorothy, took over the running of the estate, cleared the debts accumulated by Francis and Mary and improved the castle and grounds. In 1720 she created the New Way, a new, less steep approach to the castle and added a private chapel to the south front. Just before she died in 1723, she levelled the top of the tor for a bowling green and elegant brick summerhouse, perhaps used for taking tea or dessert after dinner. Nathaniel Buck's 1733 engraving (see page 40) shows her summerhouse and the New Way, lined with railings and bordered by a single line of trees. This is now a path called the Vine Walk.

Pleasure and prosperity

In 1747 Margaret Luttrell, Dorothy's granddaughter and owner of Dunster, married her cousin Henry Fownes. Henry added Luttrell to his name, becoming Henry Fownes Luttrell. Young and wealthy, they started modernising their home, ordering fashionable

Chinese painted wallpaper and putting new windows in the Dining Room and the Stair Hall. In 1755 Henry embarked on a major re-landscaping project to create a 141-hectare (348-acre) deer park at the castle, replacing the estate's former deer parks near Blue Anchor Bay.

Pleasure grounds

Henry also created new pleasure grounds below the castle. He removed the formal planting and commissioned local artist Richard Phelps to design a series of fashionable Picturesque features along the river including romantic bridges, theatrical arches and artificial waterfalls. Phelps also designed Conygar Tower and other 'ruins' on Conygar Hill, all carefully designed as eye-catchers in the view from the castle.

Right Henry Fownes Luttrell, by an unknown artist (Dining Room)

Above left Alexander Luttrell (Oak Staircase)

Above middle Dorothy Luttrell, by Michael Dahl (Dining Room)

Above right Margaret Luttrell, by Richard Phelps (Dining Room)

Reinventing the castle

In 1868, another George Luttrell initiated an ambitious programme of building at Dunster Castle. George Fownes Luttrell employed architect Anthony Salvin to redesign the castle and create a comfortable Victorian country home.

Before George inherited Dunster from his uncle in 1867, the two previous Luttrells at Dunster, John and Henry, were bachelors who preferred to live in London rather than at the castle. George's plans for Dunster were very different. George was one of nine and he had five children of his own. Agriculture was booming and the annual income from the estate, which included quarrying and forestry, was well over £22,000 – a huge amount for the time – so he had both the money and the incentive to modernise and make the castle a family home.

Modernising the castle

Salvin had worked on other castles and country houses including Alnwick, Caernarfon and Windsor Castles. At Dunster he altered the building's exterior and emphasised its medieval origins, demolishing the chapel on the south front, building two new towers and adding battlements, making it much more picturesque and irregular – looking far more convincingly like a castle. Inside he played up the early 17th-century character, adding a Jacobean-influenced library and drawing room, both with classical fireplaces. Other innovations included new bedroom suites and a bathroom with running hot water – the height of luxury!

Above The entrance front of William Arnold's Jacobean house in 1839, before Salvin's remodelling

Below Salvin's ambitious plans for Dunster were not fully realised at the request of his client

Opposite Salvin's remodelling was extensive and involved as much demolition as construction. Pictured bottom left is the only known photo of the chapel; bottom right is the hole left after it was demolished

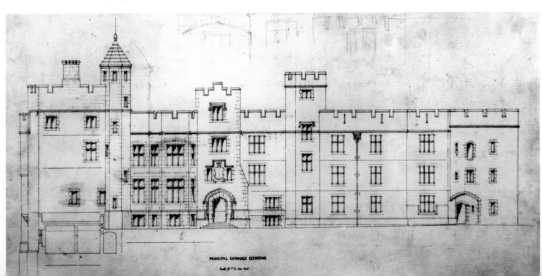

PRINCIPAL ENTRANCE ELEVATION

Improving servants' lives

A major part of Salvin's work was the enlargement and improvement of the servants' quarters. Salvin was ingenious in his designs for Dunster, recycling materials and putting in corridors so servants could move around without disturbing the family. He also relocated the kitchens from the west of the castle to a new tower wing on the east, adding levels that were partially underground. He installed central heating and gas lighting and fitted state-of-the-art cooking equipment. This worked well for all concerned, as improving the working conditions for the servants helped the Luttrells attract and retain good staff.

Function and fashion

One of Salvin's reasons for moving the kitchens was the desire to create new functional rooms for the Luttrell gentlemen – a gun room and billiard room as well as space for a study and the Luttrell archives. Billiards was a popular game and almost every country house had a billiard room.

Grandiose plans

Salvin's first proposals for the remodelling of the castle were grand and expensive, costed at £35,000. George rejected the plans and asked for decoration that was 'all plain except in the best sitting rooms'. The final bill was £25,350, quite a reduction.

Dunster in the Victorian era

With Anthony Salvin's remodelling, George and Anne Fownes Luttrell had a large comfortable country house, efficiently run with the help of servants, and had the time to be involved in local charities, politics and countryside pursuits.

Enthusiastic supporters of local commerce and industry, George and Anne backed the development of the railway to Minehead and promoted the town as a port and seaside resort. These ventures, however, were not without benefit to them, as local landowners.

A place for everything and everything in its place
Visit the Victorian kitchens on a guided tour and discover life 'below stairs'. There's lots to see with Game, Dairy and Pastry Larders, as well as the Still Room where preserves were made. Ask at the ticket office for details.

Above Salvin added the massive kitchen tower to the left of the entrance front

Far left George Fownes Luttrell, by Cyrus Johnson (Library)

Left Anne Fownes Luttrell, by Cyrus Johnson (Library)

Male and female rooms

The principal rooms in Victorian country homes were arranged into areas used predominantly by the male or female members of the family. At Dunster Castle, the Library, Dining Room, Billiard Room and Gun Room were 'male' rooms, while the Drawing Room and Morning Room were traditionally part of the 'female' domain.

A small army of servants

Strict social hierarchies in the Victorian era ruled the lives of everyone living in the castle, family and staff alike. Servants were segregated by gender, with specific jobs and areas allocated to male or female servants. The butler was in charge of male servants; the housekeeper or cook was responsible for female servants. Female staff slept at the top of the kitchen tower; male staff at the other end of the castle.

Behind the baize door

Entry into and out of the servants' quarters was through doors covered with red or green baize on the servants' side. Dunster legend has it that the colour determined who was allowed through the door. All servants could go through red doors but only certain servants such as the butler, cook, housekeeper, footmen and the Luttrells' personal servants could use the green doors that led into the formal family rooms. Housemaids would be permitted access to clean the family rooms only when they were unoccupied. Many junior servants, such as the kitchen and scullery maids, spent all their time 'below stairs' and never set eyes on the Luttrells.

Right above The Drawing Room was clearly a room designed for the pleasure and comfort of the ladies of a Victorian household

Right The kitchens designed by Salvin were part of a major renovation of the service areas by Dunster's Victorian owners

The last Luttrells at Dunster

George and Anne's son, Alexander, inherited the estate in 1910 but continued to live at Court House, East Quantoxhead. He was squire of both estates for 34 years, supporting many local organisations, including the former Minehead hospital.

A widower for more than 30 years, Alexander was highly regarded by his tenants and staff. Julian Luttrell recalls his grandfather Alexander with great affection and pride: 'He was a tangible link with the past, a peaceful, great countryman. He always wore a thick tweed suit, with a waistcoat, all year round.'

An Australian romance

Alexander's son Geoffrey met his future wife, Alys, when he was Principal Private Secretary to the Governor General of Australia. He was invited to dine with Alys' father, Admiral Bridges, an Anglo-Scot living in Victoria. Geoffrey and Alys married in 1918 and their first son, Walter, was born in 1919. They returned to England soon after and Alexander offered them Dunster.

Right above Alexander Luttrell, by Mark Milbanke (Library)

Right Geoffrey Luttrell

Far right Alys Luttrell with her children Walter, Penelope and baby Julian

Polo tournaments

Geoffrey and Alys enjoyed a busy social life with weekend shooting and hunting parties. They supported many local organisations and charities, often hosting balls and dinners. Geoffrey was interested in polo and had grounds and stabling created on the Lawns, below the castle. He hosted polo parties and tournaments, popular events watched by hundreds of spectators seated on tiered benches. He was not a polo player himself, but the sport was enthusiastically taken up by his son, Walter Luttrell, who captained the Dunster team.

Difficult times…

The Second World War brought huge political and social changes in Britain, both in town and country. The traditional role of the country squire in the 'big house' – responsible for most local employment and housing, and supporting local schools, churches and hospitals – had ended. Taxation was high, to pay for a costly war. Inheritance tax, or 'death duties' as they were known, hit estate and landowners hard.

Officers and guests

During the Second World War Alys Luttrell offered the castle as a convalescent home for the Navy. Walter Luttrell recalled that she often had 12 naval officers staying at the castle at a time. 'As soon as one went another one came in, it was absolutely choc-a-bloc.'

…difficult decisions

Times were difficult for the Luttrells. When Alexander died in 1944 the estate was liable for a huge amount of inheritance tax. Despite his advisors trying to persuade him to reduce the liability, Alexander was a principled man who believed that if tax was due it should be paid. The size of the bill left his son Geoffrey little option but to sell the castle and estate; a fate that befell many country houses at this time.

A good outcome

The castle and estate were sold to a property development company and subsequently to the Commissioners of Crown Lands. Geoffrey remained as a tenant but was able to buy back the castle and grounds in 1954. At this time the castle was opened to visitors. When he died in 1957 his widow Alys continued to live at the castle until her death in 1974. Her son, by now Lieutenant Colonel Sir Walter Luttrell, lived at East Quantoxhead, and gave Dunster Castle to the National Trust in 1976. He died in 2007.

Left Walter Luttrell with his polo team

Below Spectators in the 1930s indulging in the half-time tradition of divot stomping (treading down the torn-up turf)

From Fortress to Family Home

The castle's dramatic exterior with battlemented walls rising above a rocky outcrop belies its softer interior. Its original function was defence but, over time, this role declined as the castle evolved into a family home.

An ancient entryway

Nothing remains today of the de Mohuns' castle except the 13th-century lower-level gateway with its massive iron-bound oak doors. In the 1470s the bill for repairing the castle gateway was £1. This covered seven days' labour at 4d a day and 70lbs of iron – money clearly well spent, as the doors are still in good order today. The gatehouse through which today's visitors pass to reach the gateway was built in 1420 by Sir Hugh Luttrell.

Keeping intruders out

The medieval castle was fortified and protected by a stone curtain wall and bastion towers along the north side of the lower ward. One bastion tower remains today, although it is in a semi-ruined state. The curtain wall has gone, demolished by Cromwell's men in 1650. Parliament had ordered the destruction of the entire castle, but Thomas' son, George Luttrell, managed to persuade the authorities to let his family keep the castle.

Getting goods in

The Luttrell family still refer to the basement rooms below the Victorian kitchens as the dungeons. Salvin cleverly added a two-storey service wing behind the medieval wall, creating a back door and 'goods in' space where fresh food, coal and other household items were delivered and stored. He installed a hand-operated hoist to carry coal to each floor of the castle, saving the servants both time and effort.

Left The north front of Dunster Castle across Green Court

Right The iron-bound doors of the 13th-century gateway built by Reynold de Mohun II

Don't miss this
There is the site of an oubliette or dungeon, near the gateway. It gets its name from the French *oublier*, meaning 'to forget'. Prisoners who ended up in the oubliette were thrown in and forgotten.

The approach and porch

Most of today's visitors approach the castle as others have done for centuries: through Sir Hugh Luttrell's 15th-century gatehouse, up the stairs inside the 13th-century de Mohun gateway and across an open area known as Green Court.

This approach gives an impressive view of the castle and its main entrance on the north side with stone steps, entrance porch and tower. A watercolour of the Jacobean mansion designed by William Arnold for George Luttrell in 1617 shows a similar porch and tower, part of Arnold's design for the new house.

When Anthony Salvin remodelled Dunster Castle between 1868 and 1872 he rebuilt the entrance porch and the battlements on the roofline and added decorative stone heraldry above the entrance door. The Luttrell family motto above the entrance porch translates as 'Gained in strength, held by skill'.

The biggest change Salvin made to the previously symmetrical front elevation was to add a massive new kitchen tower to the left of the entrance. This tower is even bigger than it looks as it has another level of rooms, out of sight and partially below ground. An elegant octagonal turret houses the staircase for the new tower.

Above The area between the gateway and the north front known as Green Court

The Outer and Inner Halls

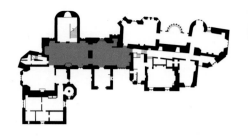

The Inner Hall was the Great Hall and core of the Jacobean mansion built in 1617. Salvin created the Outer Hall in 1870 from three rooms in the old mansion, removing a mezzanine floor to give it added height.

In Victorian times guests were welcomed in the Outer Hall by footmen in uniform. The two rooms that Salvin took out on the south side of the Outer Hall originally led into the chapel built for Dorothy Luttrell in the early 1700s. The chapel was removed as part of Salvin's redesign of the castle, when he added the new Drawing Room Tower to the south front.

All that remains of George Luttrell's Jacobean decoration of the Great Hall is a plasterwork ceiling and the fireplace overmantel, with the coats of arms of his parents Thomas and Margaret Luttrell.

Salvin installed a huge baronial chimneypiece in the Inner Hall. It is carved with an inscription from the Domesday Book entry for Dunster referring to the land of William de Mohun. Salvin also removed the arches in the Inner Hall and installed Jacobean-style ones instead.

The painting between the arches is a 1591 copy of Hans Eworth's highly unusual portrait of Sir John Luttrell painted about 1550, full of symbolism. It may refer to the peace treaty of 1550, by which France recovered the port of Boulogne from England (the woman holding the olive branch probably represents Peace). John Luttrell had helped to capture Boulogne in 1544 and seems, with shaking fist, to be opposing its return. The storm-tossed ship may be the *Mary of Hamburg,* which was badly damaged in the evacuation of Inchcolm Island in the Firth of Forth, where Luttrell commanded a small fleet. The Latin inscriptions in the rock and on his bracelet praise Luttrell's courage.

Left The Inner Hall in about 1910

Far left The strongly symbolic portrait of Sir John Luttrell

The Drawing Room

This formal room occupies the ground floor of the tower that Salvin added to the south front. It is deliberately asymmetrical, with large and small bay windows, where quiet conversations could be held in some privacy.

This was where the family had morning refreshment and entertained local gentry paying social calls. In fine weather, they would move to the terrace. Family and guests also gathered here before and after dinner. The women often withdrew to this room after dinner to chat and enjoy a cup of coffee or glass of wine together before the men rejoined them.

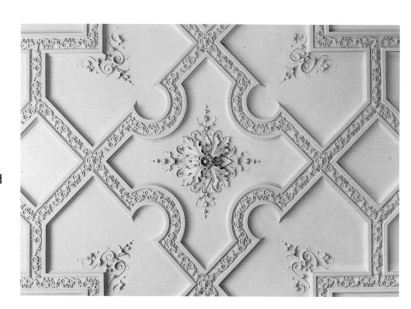

Salvin planned the decoration of this room from ceiling to floor. He designed the neo-Jacobean ceiling, the frieze of which incorporates the 'GL' of George Fownes Luttrell, who commissioned the room. Salvin also installed the brass gasolier, which was later converted to electricity. His elaborate parquetry floor, with its geometric inlay, has survived many decorative schemes over the years. Alys Luttrell used this room for formal afternoon tea. She had it redecorated in 1935, replacing the Victorian wallpaper with panels in fashionable eau-de-nil colour.

Above The plasterwork of Salvin's neo-Jacobean ceiling

Left A servants' bell pull in the Drawing Room

Opposite The Drawing Room

The Dining Room and Servery

Francis and Mary Luttrell redesigned the Dining Room in the 1680s. Its elaborate plasterwork ceiling and wall frieze were a bold statement of their wealth and status. The Luttrell coat of arms is above the fireplace, Mary's family crest in the frieze.

Mary used the adjoining room as an intimate withdrawing room in which to entertain her most favoured guests. When Salvin redesigned this space with efficiency in mind, he changed this room into a servery, where trays of food brought up from the kitchens could be put down until all could be served together.

Salvin added the Dining Room's bay window and its plasterwork ceiling, inspired by that of the original room. He also installed a speaking tube between the Butler's Pantry and the Kitchen. Whilst functionality was key, he left the spectacular plasterwork ceiling with its swirls of fruits, leaves and animals as well as putti, or cherubs. This is probably the work of Edward Goudge, described in 1690 as 'ye beste master in England in his profession'.

The last Luttrells at Dunster used this room every day. Breakfast and lunch were served at a round table in the window, dinner on the main table. Julian Luttrell remembers Christmas meals with crested Wedgwood plates, silver candelabra, colourful Hock glasses, Waterford crystal, silver cutlery and 'masses of crackers'.

Dinner for the Maharajah

Exotic curry spices and ingredients from Fortnum and Mason were ordered for a grand dinner held for the Maharajah of Jaipur and his polo team in 1935. Geoffrey Luttrell considered it the most expensive dinner he hosted, because guests drank huge quantities of wine to quell the heat of the curry!

The Pantry Lobby and Butler's Pantry

The Pantry Lobby and Butler's Pantry were built by Salvin as part of his new kitchen tower in the 1870s. Dunster Castle was a home that was lived in up until 1974, and these rooms in particular show how a medieval castle was modified for modern living.

Since Salvin's kitchen tower was constructed in the 1870s, these rooms have been modest but functionally important spaces. The best silver was cleaned in the plate-cleaning room off the Pantry Lobby and was stored in the adjacent plate safe. A mechanical lift, known as a dumbwaiter, brought serving dishes and food up from the kitchens below.

Around 1962, when the widowed Alys Luttrell was living in the castle, a modern kitchen was installed in the Butler's Pantry, now known as the 'new kitchen'. Alys' son, Sir Walter, installed the new kitchen while she was visiting Australia. Although pleased with the kitchen, Alys was saddened by the changes in society it represented and initially instructed her cook to continue using the old Victorian cooking range. Her 'modern' kitchen represents another example of the different periods of history that can be seen at Dunster Castle.

Opposite The Dining Room with the Servery beyond

Right The new kitchen brings the story of Dunster's long occupation up to date

The Stair Hall

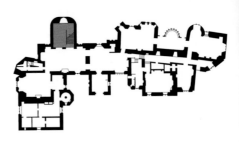

This carved staircase is one of Dunster Castle's special treasures. Installed by Francis and Mary Luttrell in the 1680s, it is an outstanding piece of craftsmanship, probably by Edward Pearce, one of the best carvers of the time.

False symmetry

There are two matching doors on the landing at the top of the carved staircase but only one of them is real. A false door was built here in 1772–73 to give the landing a symmetrical appearance. This was part of the redecoration undertaken by Henry Fownes Luttrell.

Today the staircase is a feast for the eyes in rich, dark wood, but at one time all this intricate carving was painted white.

Each panel is carved from a single piece of elm, cleverly linked by curling acanthus leaves that draw the eye up the staircase. The panels are carved with hunting scenes that run in and out of the acanthus leaves, demonstrating the Luttrell family's love of country sports. There are also piles of money – Charles II shillings and Turkish, Irish and Portuguese coins, reflecting contemporary history and trading links.

The ceiling of the staircase has ornate plasterwork with hunting scenes and a flowing scroll of acanthus leaves, as in the staircase panels. It was made at the same time as the elaborate plasterwork ceiling in the Dining Room.

Left **The Stair Hall**

Right **The carved balustrade features intriguing details including Charles II silver shillings**

The Morning Room

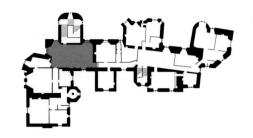

This room has had various uses and names over the centuries. In 1675 it was the Red Chamber, in 1772 the Breakfast Room, in 1867 the Morning Room and in the Luttrells' 1974 guidebook it was called the Great Parlour.

It was remodelled in Henry Fownes Luttrell's time, when the Georgian fireplace, doors, dado and cornice were put in. Alys Luttrell used it as her sitting room, complete with large television set. Now it is a place where visitors can relax and find out more about the castle and its history.

The Morning Room is surprisingly modest after the grandeur of the carved staircase. It is likely that Francis and Mary planned that the stairs should lead to an equally sumptuous room. However that didn't happen, perhaps because they had run out of money after all their lavish spending or, more likely, because Francis died unexpectedly aged only 31, and his widow had to quit the castle.

Four early 18th-century paintings hanging on the walls of the Morning Room show the countryside around the castle at that time. They make for fascinating study, showing what has changed and what has remained the same in the area surrounding Dunster.

Right The four early 18th-century paintings of the surrounding countryside make interesting comparisons with today's views from the Morning Room

The Wisteria Bedroom and Passage

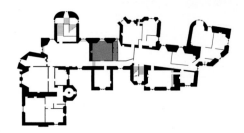

This room gets its name from the wisteria that climbed up the wall outside its window. When George Fownes Luttrell inherited the castle in 1867 and brought his family of five children to Dunster, there was an urgent need for more bedrooms.

The two previous owners had both been bachelors, so part of Salvin's commission was to provide bedrooms for the family and visiting relations.

The wallpaper dates from the late 19th century, but the rest of the furniture was not originally in this room. In a 1910 inventory this room is called 'Late Mr Luttrell's Room'.

After George's death this room became a guest room, perhaps because of its splendid views over the castle gardens and parkland. It was next to the only bathroom in this part of the house, which was shared with the neighbouring East Quantoxhead Bedroom.

The room was partially redecorated when the washbasin was installed in the 1930s, while Geoffrey and Alys Luttrell were living at Dunster. Favoured guests were given this room when they stayed for Dunster's popular shooting and polo parties.

Below The 19th-century wallpaper with floral design in the Wisteria Bedroom

The East Quantoxhead Suite

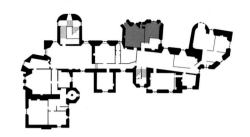

This bedroom is named after the Luttrells' other Somerset estate at the nearby village of East Quantoxhead. However the 1910 inventory lists this room as 'Mrs Luttrell's Bedroom' and its adjoining dressing room as 'Mrs Luttrell's Sitting Room'.

Salvin installed the cast-iron bath with its mahogany surround in the 1870s. He also put in the fireplace, which is made of red marble from Torquay. When it was put in this was the only bathroom in the castle. Prior to this innovation the family bathed in their bedrooms, in hip baths. Servants had to carry jugs of hot and cold water up to the bedrooms – an exhausting and time-consuming task.

When Geoffrey and Alys Luttrell moved into the castle in 1920, they had this suite of rooms redecorated and modernised, replacing the Victorian fireplace in the bedroom. Today the bedroom is laid out in the style of the 1930s, although only the dressing table and the curtains are original. The colourful quilt on the bed was 'worked by the Miss Luttrells of Dunster Castle about 1830'. These are believed to have been three spinster sisters, Mary, Margaret and Harriet.

Above **The East Quantoxhead Bedroom**

Left Servants could be summoned by bell pulls and handles in the guest suites and throughout the castle

The Leather Gallery

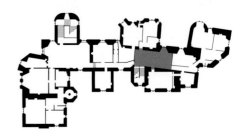

These painted leather hangings are arguably the rarest and most important pieces in Dunster's collection. They are the only collection of leather hangings of this type in the United Kingdom.

They tell the love story of a Roman general, Antony, and an Egyptian queen, Cleopatra, a tale made famous by Shakespeare. Made of calf-skin, the hangings are embossed and painted to give a three-dimensional appearance.

The scenes were probably made in the Netherlands in the late 1600s, but they were not commissioned for Dunster, and were altered to fit this room. First hung here sometime between

1701 and 1741, they were cut up and moved around to fit the available space, like grand wallpaper, hence the haphazard order of the story.

By 1704 this room was the formal banqueting room and the leather hangings would have been both impressive and practical. Leather hangings were often chosen for dining rooms as, unlike fabric, leather does not retain food smells. They were repaired in 1759 and re-hung again in the 1870s.

The fine set of chairs and settee were bought for Dunster before 1781. A photograph shows them here before Salvin remodelled this room.

Opposite The gilt leather hangings depict the story of Antony and Cleopatra; here Octavius Caesar and Lepidus with Mark Antony

Far left Here Antony receives Cleopatra

Left The tragic end of the story of Antony and Cleopatra's love affair was her death from the venomous bite of an asp

The King Charles Room
The Oak Staircase

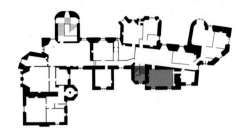

The King Charles Room

The future King Charles II stayed at Dunster in 1645 while raising support for the Royalist cause. He is thought to have slept in this part of the castle and this bedroom has been known as 'King Charles' Room' since the 19th century. Family tradition has it that the secret door beside the bed led to an escape ladder.

This was always a principal bedroom. In 1690 it was the White Chamber, the most expensively furnished, with 'Gold coloured Mohair lined with blew Sarsenett' bed hangings, a suite of japanned (imitating Asian lacquer work) furniture, white curtains, and a set of tapestries. In 1741 it was the Yellow Chamber with yellow curtains and upholstery, and in 1781 the Red Room with crimson curtains. In the 19th century it was furnished with carved dark oak furniture, and wallpaper designed by Pugin and produced by the prestigious decorating firm Crace & Son. Perry & Coles reprinted it in 1991 using the original wooden printing blocks.

Left This warming pan commemorates the occasion on which it is thought the future King Charles II slept in this room

Above Finely carved furniture in the King Charles Room. The commemorative wallpaper was reprinted using the original blocks

The oversized plasterwork overmantel is dated 1602 and locally made. Based on a Flemish engraving it depicts *The Judgement of Paris*. The prince of Troy, Paris, was asked to choose which of three goddesses was the most beautiful. He awarded the prize – a golden apple – to Aphrodite, who promised him the world's most beautiful woman, Helen, wife of the Greek King Menelaus. The Greeks' attempt to rescue Helen caused the Trojan War.

Above The Judgement of Paris overmantel was moved here from a room with a much larger fireplace

The Oak Staircase

This is Dunster's secondary staircase, giving access to the upper floors. The upper section is partly early 17th-century, but lower flights have elegant turned balusters made about 1700.

These stairs were used by the family and servants. Victorian convention ruled that servants, especially lower servants such as housemaids, were not to be seen by the family. They must have had some frustrating times, waiting for a suitable opportunity to run, unseen, up or downstairs to do their work.

On the east (right-hand) wall hang 12 engravings of William Hogarth's famous mid-18th-century satirical paintings.

Ghostly goings on

This bedroom is said to be the most haunted room in the castle, with many visitors commenting on a feeling of unease. Julian Luttrell remembers how his father and a friend hid in the secret passage and made ghostly noises to scare a guest staying in the King Charles Bedroom. Their giggles gave them away.

The Gun Room
The Billiard Room

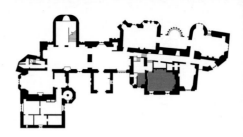

The Gun Room

The Gun Room was built as part of Salvin's Victorian 'male' suite of rooms with the Justice Room, Billiard Room and Library. It was a busy, bustling place used by the men of the family and by servants.

The servants cleaned, serviced and stored the guns, which were collected and dropped off here by the family and their guests. Luggage was also delivered here and taken to the bedrooms via the stairs and passageways that lead off to the other service areas of the Victorian castle.

Many of the Luttrell family were keen sportsmen, passionate about hunting and shooting. Geoffrey was an enthusiastic shot and in the 1920s and 1930s the Gun Room was kept busy with numerous shooting parties. It still looks much as it did in his day, with its muted green walls and original fixtures of gun racks, leather straps and the gun cupboard.

The muskets on the wall date from the 1670s and 1680s. They are part of the collection of muskets that Colonel Francis Luttrell gathered together when he was in charge of the local militia after the Civil War. Some of the muskets in the Gun Room are carved with 'FL', Francis Luttrell's initials.

A day's sport
Colonel Sir Walter Luttrell was a very keen huntsman. While he was a student at Oxford he would leave for Dunster early in the morning, arriving in time for breakfast, hunt all day with this beagles (here he's photographed surrounded by them), have a quick supper and then drive 140 miles back to Oxford before his college shut the gates.

The Billiard Room

Almost every Victorian country house had a billiard room where the family and their guests spent many enjoyable hours. Initially it was just a game for men, but by the end of the 19th century women were also playing billiards.

Dunster's Billiard Room is well equipped with a high-quality table, scoreboard and other accessories supplied by Burroughs & Watts, a famous Victorian company. Originally the billiard balls were made of ivory, which came from elephant tusks. Hand-made, they varied in weight and size, adding an extra degree of difficulty to the game. Salvin created this room in what had been the kitchen of the Jacobean house. Before this there had been a billiard table in the Inner Hall. He kept the stone fireplace arch of the cooking range, and installed a much smaller grate so he could add seating to either side. Salvin also re-used columns and doors that he had removed from the Inner Hall and Dining Room.

Below The Billiard Room

Left Shotguns in the gun cupboard

The Muniment Rooms, Justice Room and Library Passage

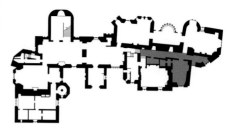

These rooms and the passage were part of Salvin's remodelling of the castle between 1868 and 1872. The Justice Room was created for George Fownes Luttrell, to provide him with a quiet study, away from the bustle and noise of the family rooms.

Salvin designed the Muniment Rooms to store the Luttrell archives – the legal and historical records relating to the castle and the estate. The archives are extensive and at that time required two rooms. They were stored here until 1958 when they were transferred to the County Records Office. They are still stored by the county, at the Somerset Heritage Centre in Taunton.

The archives cover centuries of the family's history at Dunster. Fortunately they survived the troubled times during the Civil War when the castle was besieged by Parliamentarians. The family papers were reorganised in 1650, just after the Civil War, and were subsequently re-catalogued in the early 20th century by the historian Sir Henry Maxwell Lyte.

The Justice Room did not have a formal judicial role, although several of the Luttrells were Justices of the Peace. Estate tenants who came to discuss matters with their landlord could approach the Justice Room discreetly from a nearby outside door. The Library Passage links all the 'male' rooms of the castle – the Billiard Room, the Muniment Rooms, the Justice Room and the new Library.

Left The Justice Room

The Library

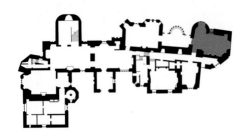

Dunster's Library is the highlight of Salvin's 'male' Victorian rooms. The Luttrell men relaxed here, chatting, playing cards and games and reading their papers and books.

This room was created from three smaller rooms and extended into a mezzanine floor for extra height. Salvin probably designed the bookcases, but the upper shelves are later. They hold an eclectic collection of books, reflecting the family's interests in country sports, history and gardening. The most famous book associated with the Luttrells is the *Luttrell Psalter*, a 14th-century illuminated manuscript. The original is in the British Library, but there is a Victorian facsimile edition in Dunster's Library.

The comfortable maroon leather chairs and settees are listed in the inventory of 1910, and are typical furnishings for such a room.

Below The Library's collection of books reflects the wide-ranging interests of the Luttrells

The wallpaper features exotic birds called hoopoes and dates from the late 19th century, when there was a fashion for embossed paper in the style of leather hangings. In 1994 sections of the wallpaper were repaired and cleaned by specialist conservators. They painstakingly removed and re-used sections of paper from behind the paintings as these were in good condition, having been protected from sunlight.

Paintings

Around the Library are portraits of 19th- and 20th-century Luttrells. The twice-decorated and one-eyed gentleman in his red 1st Foot Guards uniform is Lieutenant Colonel Francis Luttrell, painted in 1855. Francis' battalion played a decisive part in the Battle of Waterloo in 1815, driving back Napoleon's Imperial Guard at a crucial moment. To the left of the fireplace is his nephew George Fownes Luttrell, who inherited Dunster from his other uncle, Henry, in 1867. To the right of the fireplace is George's wife, Anne Elizabeth Hood, and above the door is their son, Alexander Fownes Luttrell. Over the fireplace is Alexander's son, Geoffrey Fownes Luttrell.

Above **The Library in about 1910**

Left above **The embossed 19th-century wallpaper features hoopoes, colourful birds notable for their distinctive crown of feathers**

Left **Lieutenant Colonel Francis Luttrell (1792–1862), by Ensign W. Barrett**

The Conservatory

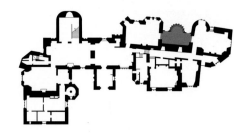

Conservatories were fashionable features of large Victorian country houses. Salvin's Conservatory creates a light and airy link between the Library and the Drawing Room, and makes the most of the view to the south.

The Conservatory also links two of the key Victorian 'male' and 'female' rooms – the rich and boldly colourful 'male' Library, and the more delicately furnished 'female' Drawing Room.

The patterned terracotta floor tiles were made by Minton's Ltd, the famous tile company in Stoke on Trent.

In summer the Conservatory is fragrant with the perfume of flowers growing in its sheltered microclimate. It is a perfect spot to sit and admire the view over the terraced gardens to the rolling Exmoor landscape with its fields, woodland and moorland.

Above The view from the Conservatory towards the deer park

Opposite The Conservatory offered lightness and fragrance after the gloomier, smoke-filled interior of the Library

Left The Conservatory in about 1910

An Historic Garden and Estate

The steep slopes around Dunster Castle have been cultivated since the 1700s. Remnants of former planting schemes give clues of changing fashions in landscaping and horticulture stretching over four centuries.

Gardens of many aspects

As comfort and appearance became higher priorities than defence, and sharing the views from the castle became more important than keeping avaricious eyes out, the gardens were developed into a place to delight the senses with artful planting and the remarkable views afforded from the tor.

Today the gardens are known for their diversity of plants and features, with sub-tropical, Mediterranean and temperate plants beside the river, in herbaceous borders and the terraced gardens. The castle grounds are also famous for their spectacular views over the Somerset countryside and the waters of the Bristol Channel. The Lawns, 20th-century polo grounds, lie below the gardens, surrounded by the Dunster estate. Its farmland, woods, forests and quarries are all now managed by the Crown Estates.

'This site, with its extraordinary variety of aspect, exposure, soil conditions and moisture, creates unmatched opportunity for the plantsman, inspiration for the designer and challenge for the gardener; and it is the setting for a garden of astonishing diversity'

'A Garden of Many Parts', *Country Life*, 1990

Left The variety of terrain around the castle creates gardens each with very a different character and planting

Above The Keep Garden is home to traditional English bedding plants

Opposite The slopes around Dunster pose some significant gardening challenges

The garden through time

Records from 1543 refer to a walled kitchen garden east of Dunster church, but there is nothing left of this today. There are, however, the remains of landscape designs from each of the last four centuries as well as exciting 21st-century features.

Very little is known about the appearance of any garden at Dunster Castle in the Middle Ages. George Luttrell had commissioned William Arnold to create a Jacobean mansion in the castle buildings but we don't know where or what its gardens were.

Nathaniel Buck's *North East View of Dunster Castle* of 1733 shows the New Way and the slopes just below the castle formally planted with rows of shrubs, possibly topiary – old yews still survive. The motte – the mound where the castle keep had stood – had formal planting and a flattened top, now the Keep Garden, surrounded by a wall enclosing a bowling green and summerhouse created by

Dorothy Luttrell. George Wood's painting of 1735 shows a large walled formal garden below the castle in the park near the river, with a straight central walk, a pavilion and an open loggia. It was altered at some point; a plan of about 1750 shows a central round pool. Archaeological investigation has found many traces of this garden.

Above Dunster Castle in its Picturesque pleasure grounds, by John Nixon *c.*1780

Below Nathaniel Buck's view of the castle and garden in 1733 shows the gatehouse on the right and the recently built octagonal summerhouse on the top of the levelled tor

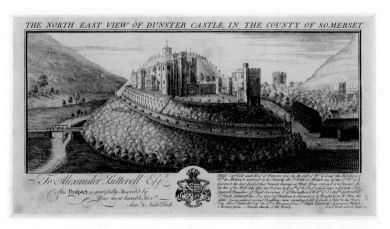

THE NORTH EAST VIEW OF DUNSTER CASTLE, IN THE COUNTY OF SOMERSET.

Creating the pleasure grounds

Henry Fownes Luttrell instigated major changes to the castle's parkland and gardens. In 1755 he created a new larger deer park at the castle, replacing two older, smaller parks near Blue Anchor Bay.

Accommodating the new deer park, just south of the castle, involved evicting several tenant farmers. Their leases were cancelled, hedges removed and a strong, wooden fence was built to contain the deer. When the deer were moved to their new home villagers from Dunster, Carhampton and Withycombe lined the route from the old deer parks so none could escape.

In 1775 Henry commissioned Richard Phelps to develop Picturesque-style gardens. Lawns' and Lovers' Bridges and the rocky cascade on the River Avill were the result, along with the folly, Conygar Tower.

Faded glory

By 1830 the sloping ground around the castle was covered with evergreen shrubs and trees including laurels. The castle was inherited by two bachelor brothers, neither of whom chose to live at Dunster. They did however open up the castle grounds to visitors. In 1845 an Elizabeth Ernst recorded: 'The present state of the castle exhibits a sad picture of departed greatness.'

Victorian order

Things changed dramatically when George Fownes Luttrell moved to Dunster. As well as redesigning the castle, he had an underground water reservoir constructed beneath the Keep Garden to store water for the castle and village. His staff created an impressive Victorian garden with formal terraces and colourful, regimented borders.

Above Conygar Tower was part of Henry Fownes Luttrell's Picturesque pleasure grounds

Left Lovers' Bridge is consciously Picturesque with pointed arches, rock-faced stonework and a seat for two

The last one hundred years

Dunster's gardens offer the gardening team as many rewards as they present challenges. The team not only works on the many historical layers of the gardens, but their work is often on very steep slopes, adding a whole new dimension to tasks.

The occasionally steep terrain makes the site vulnerable to erosion, especially after heavy rain. However, the complexity of the design – gardens within a garden – means a surprising variety of plants can be grown here.

Changing uses

The Keep Garden was made into a tennis court in the 1920s, soon after Geoffrey and Alys Luttrell moved into the castle. Alys Luttrell was an enthusiastic gardener and left her mark on Dunster, especially in the River Garden where she introduced exotic semi-tropical plants that thrive in the damp atmosphere. Alys also created a garden in the walled garden near the Stables, now redeveloped as the Dream Garden in commemoration of her love of colour. Over the five decades that Alys lived at Dunster the gardens were often opened to raise funds for local charities including the Red Cross.

Left A glimpse of the sea from the Keep Garden with sun-loving cistus in the foreground

Above The Terrace Gardens are home to plants more common to the Mediterranean than Minehead

Far right The River Gardens have their own microclimate supporting sub-tropical plants

Right The Dream Garden is a new creation celebrating Alys Luttrell's love of colour

Diverse aspects

The castle grounds cover almost seven hectares and have different gardens within that area, reflecting the varied microclimates of the tor. The River Gardens are a special feature with sub-tropical plants, including the enormous gunnera that you cannot fail to see, all thriving in the moisture-laden atmosphere along the River Avill. In contrast, the south-facing Terrace Gardens are home to sun-loving, drought-resistant Mediterranean plants.

Sustainable gardening

Today the National Trust looks after the grounds at Dunster with just four staff and the help of volunteers, unlike Victorian times when there were many more gardeners. The Trust takes a sustainable approach, using plants that can flourish without frequent watering and chemical fertilisers.

Inspiring vision

The Trust is restoring the gardens' historic views and features. Diseased and over-mature trees and shrubs are being removed, and a new winter border has been created with thousands of crocus and hyacinth bulbs beside the former Magnolia Walk. Shrubs on the steep slopes are being pruned to create a carpet of evergreen, punctuated by pockets of planting adding colour and interest. In the River Gardens there's a rustic log play area created from a fallen conifer.

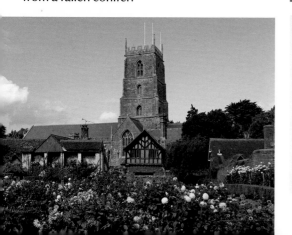

Tall tales

Sir Walter Luttrell remembered an early tour guide, Harold Owens, telling wonderfully outrageous stories to visitors to the castle gardens in the 1920s. Wisteria and a lemon tree grow against the south front: the wisteria was apparently thousands of years old, and the lemon tree grew in height each time he described it.

The Stables

Right The view through the gatehouse to the Stables

Far right Dunster's working watermill

Left The Stables date from the 17th century and have the original stalls

Below Alys with her groom Reg Godvey and Jigsaw

Dunster's stables are very grand, dating from the early 17th century. They are one of the earliest-surviving stable blocks owned by the National Trust. The interior is complete, with its original stalls, including unusual hanging partitions.

The Stables may have been built for George Luttrell, but their date of construction is unknown. A Civil War cannon ball found in the stable rafters makes it likely the Stables were built before 1645.

Horses were a vital source of transport and power for farming and industry before motor vehicles were invented. Horsemanship was a prestigious skill, the mark of a gentleman. Many of the Luttrells were keen sportsmen, enjoying countryside pursuits, especially hunting. Geoffrey Luttrell had polo grounds established on the Lawns and arranged

tournaments each year. Two Indian Maharajahs and their polo teams were invited, including that of the Maharajah of Jodhpur in 1928. The Maharajah arrived with his cook and servants as well as a string of 62 ponies, each with their own groom, and they all stayed in purpose-built stables beside the polo lawns.

Alys Luttrell was a keen horsewoman and she loved riding and driving a carriage pulled by Jigsaw, her skewbald high-stepping trap pony. Jigsaw is buried on the edge of the park, just below the path to Lawns' Bridge. Reg Godvey was her groom for 35 years and lived in a flat above the Stables.

Championship cider
During the 1920s an area of the Stables was used to make cider, which was sold to local residents and nearby pubs and inns. Cider made in Dunster's stables won the All England Cider Championship in 1928.

The Mill

The Domesday Book records a mill at Dunster Castle in 1086, and a mill stands on the same site beside the River Avill today. The current buildings date from 1779 when they were rebuilt and updated with French machinery and new millstones.

The Mill was abandoned sometime before the 1930s, but refurbished in 1942 during the Second World War to mill animal feed, and it continued to operate until 1962. Rescued from disuse by Mr Capps, who restored it to working order in 1972, it is one of the finest working watermills in the West Country.

Mills were a vital part of everyday life for centuries. There were mills on most rivers in England, often several on a mile of river, all providing power to drive machinery. Dunster's Mill was a corn mill, grinding corn and other grains into flour for baking and cooking. Other mills were used to drive machinery such as saws at timber mills and quarries, or pumps to remove water from underground mines.

The Keepers of the Castle

Striking the balance between conserving the castle and enabling people to enjoy its special character and collections is a constant challenge. The National Trust's central ethos of 'For ever, for everyone' creates a dynamic tension.

Encouraging more visitors puts additional pressure on the historic fabric of the buildings. Opening the collections more frequently increases their exposure to sunlight and susceptibility to wear and tear. All heritage sites face these challenges, and the Trust's team strives to meet them imaginatively and successfully.

Occupying a central role

The castle has been the centre of a great country estate for centuries, a constant feature in local people's lives. It's also been a much-loved family home, full of special stories and memories for many generations. Setting the castle in its historic context is important. Sir Walter and Julian Luttrell were the last young men to be brought up at the castle, and their help in presenting the castle as a home has been invaluable.

The castle is also a key part of the tourist economy, and the Trust works with local organisations and is involved in regional initiatives to attract visitors to the area. A joint initiative with the West Somerset

Railway, the Dunster Castle Express, is reviving a traditional way of travelling to the castle. This also helps reduce traffic in West Somerset and eases pressure on parking in the village.

Thinking sustainably

Dunster Castle was the National Trust's first Grade I Listed Building to install photovoltaic solar panels, with over 100 positioned on the castle roof. It is a good location, well aligned for catching sunlight and out of sight from visitors and local residents. The Trust is investigating re-commissioning the Victorian water reservoir under the Keep Garden to provide water for the toilets and to irrigate the gardens.

The bottom line

Each year the National Trust undertakes vital conservation and maintenance work at Dunster Castle and in the surrounding grounds. Funding this work is expensive and ongoing. To invest in Dunster we have to be commercially competent and ensure our customers are satisfied and support our work. Every visitor and every purchase – including this guidebook! – help to protect the castle for future generations.

Opposite Dunster Castle flies the flag for sustainability. The roof has over 100 photovoltaic solar panels generating electricity

Above and left A visit to Dunster Castle is much more than a history lesson

A shared view

'I hope you have enjoyed discovering more about Dunster Castle, its people and some of the key moments in its history. It's a remarkable survivor, withstanding the ravages of war, of politics and economics, transformed over the centuries by fate and fortune.

Like many people I never cease to be struck by the magnificence of the castle's setting. Who could drive along the A39 and not be drawn to look across to this stunning building, sprouting up from its tor, at one with the landscape around it? The weather and light combine to ensure the view never looks the same twice. I speculate that it was the castle's setting that has resulted in its survival: in its day an impenetrable fortress, and then a residence commanding unrivalled outlooks, surveying the great estate that surrounded it with a benign dignity. This commanding location has afforded it a special significance and means it was never to be abandoned or left to ruin.

Dunster gets under your skin and hopefully part of the magic of the place has spoken from these pages. I hope you, your families and friends will visit us many times in the future to enjoy all that Dunster Castle has to offer, or even join our dedicated band of volunteers and help us to assure its survival for another thousand years.'

Seamus Rogers, General Manager

Above Dunster Castle, still standing after a thousand years